Main Idea

Reading Comprehension Book
Reading Level 2.0–3.5

Introduction

Welcome to the Edupress Main Idea Reading Comprehension Book. This resource is an effective tool for instruction, practice, and evaluation of student understanding. It includes ideas on how to introduce identifying the main idea to students, as well as activities to help teach and practice the concept.

The reproducible activities in this book are tailored to individual, small-group, and whole-class work. They include leveled reading passages, graphic organizers, worksheets, and detailed instruction pages. These activities provide opportunities to use text, illustrations, graphics, and combinations of these elements to practice finding the main idea in texts.

The material in this book is written for readers at the 2.0–3.5 reading level. However, the activities can easily be adapted to your students' ability levels and your time frame. After introducing an activity to students, model it by working through one or two examples aloud. You may wish to also read text passages aloud to students, or they can be read silently or aloud by students. For students who need personalized help, individual and small-group activities have been included. These activities can be done alone or with a classroom aide for explicit instruction.

We know you will be pleased with the progress your students make in identifying main ideas after using this book.

EP2364 © 2010 Demco, Inc. • 4810 Forest Run Road • Madison, WI 53704

ISBN 13: 978-1-56472-154-9

www.edupressinc.com

Table of Contents

Directions: Details in Brief

Individual

As a class, discuss the concept of finding the main idea and why it is an important reading comprehension skill. Reproduce the In Two Words Graphic Organizer on page 4 for each student. Tell students they can only use two words to describe each experience on the graphic organizer. For example, for "What I did last weekend," students might write "Dad's house" or "went swimming." Explain how this exercise will help them narrow down a lot of information into one main idea.

Small Group

Have students divide into pairs. Reproduce the In Two Words Graphic Organizer for each student. Instruct students to interview each other to fill in their graphic organizers. Have students use their partners' responses to write two words in each box. After each student has been interviewed, have students show their graphic organizers to each other. Do the two-word answers properly convey the main idea? As an extension, challenge students to make their own graphic organizers with different questions.

In Two Words Graphic Organizer

Name:

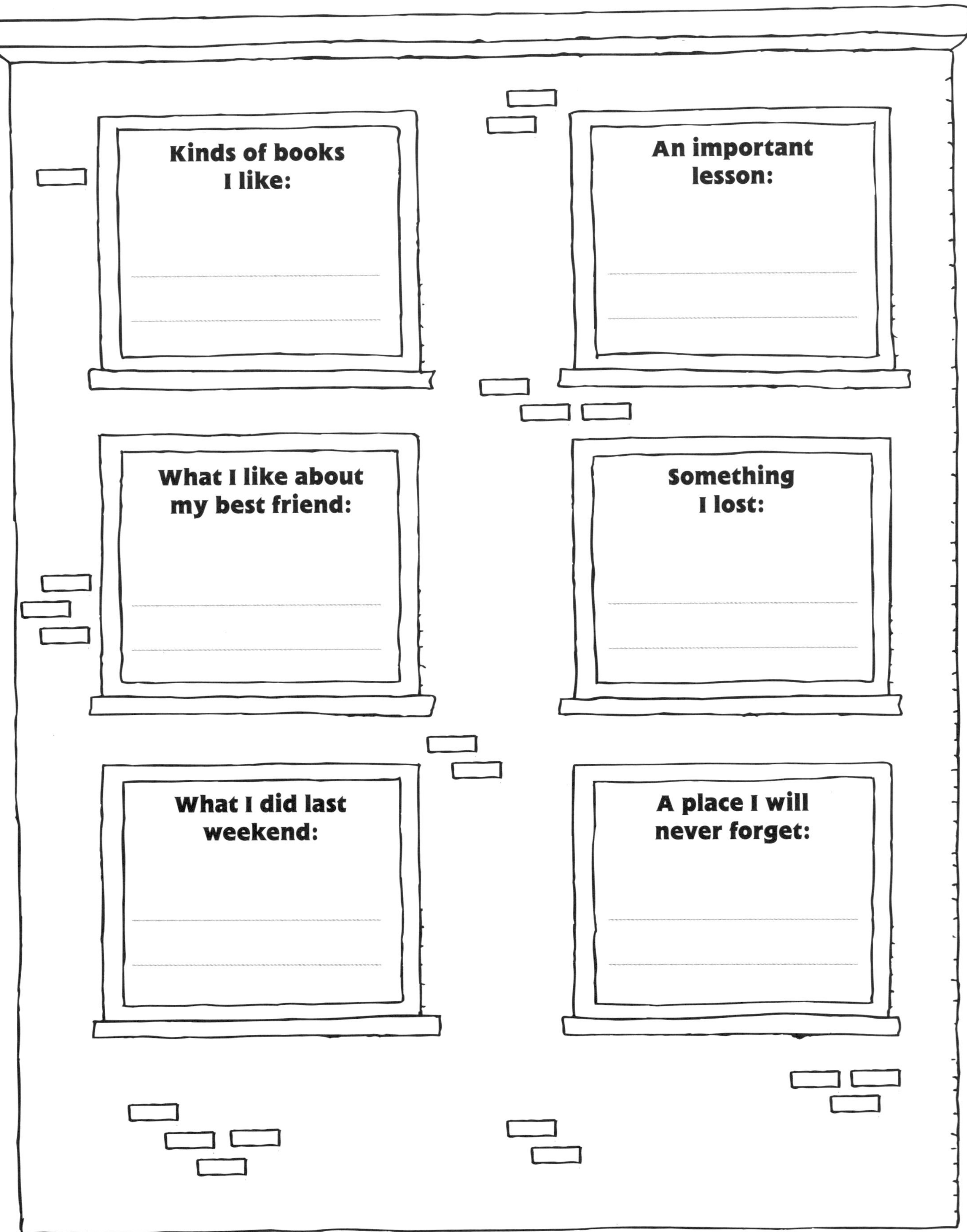

Directions: Picture Puzzles

Individual

Reproduce Main Idea Puzzles 1 and 2 on pages 6 and 7 for each student. Instruct students to write a sentence describing the main idea of each picture. Then, ask them to think about the main idea of all three pictures as a set. Invite students to share their ideas during a class discussion. How were answers alike and different?

As an extension, invite students to find three related pictures in old magazines, newspapers, or junk mail. Encourage them to cut out the pictures, mount them on a sheet of colored paper, and add a title or a main idea sentence.

Small Group

Divide the class into groups of three. Reproduce one of the Main Idea Puzzle pages for each group. Cut the pictures apart, and give each student one picture. Each student should write down the main idea of his or her picture. Then, have students determine as a group the main idea of the picture set. When all groups are finished, discuss the answers as a class.

Whole Class

Reproduce the Main Idea Puzzles on transparencies. Divide the class into two teams. Show one picture at a time on the overhead. Give a point to the first team who can correctly say the main idea of each picture. After you have shown all three pictures, give five points to the first team who can say what all pictures in the set have in common (the main idea). The team with the most points after showing all the pictures wins.

Answer Key (suggested answers)

Main Idea Puzzles 1 (Page 6)

Picture 1 Main Idea: A train travels through the countryside.

Picture 2 Main Idea: Cars drive through the country.

Picture 3 Main Idea: An airplane flies over the countryside.

Main Idea of all three pictures: There are many ways to get from place to place.

Main Idea Puzzles 2 (Page 7)

Picture 1 Main Idea: A girl sees an airplane fly over her house.

Picture 2 Main Idea: A deer watches a large bird fly over the mountains.

Picture 3 Main Idea: A ladybug watches a bee fly over some flowers.

Main Idea of all three pictures: There are many things that fly.

Main Idea Puzzles 1

Name: ______

1

Main Idea: ______

2

Main Idea: ______

3

Main Idea: ______

Main Idea Puzzles 2

Name: ______________________

1

Main Idea: ______________________

2

Main Idea: ______________________

3

Main Idea: ______________________

Directions: Reading for the Main Idea

Individual ●

Reproduce "Country Summer" on page 9 or "Paulo's Birthday Pizza" on page 11 and its matching graphic organizer on page 10 or 12 for each student. Encourage students to read the stories carefully. Then, have students fill in the graphic organizers.

Help them think of the main idea by reminding them to come up with just two words to describe the story. This will help them narrow their focus.

When all students have finished, invite volunteers to share their graphic organizers with the class. Display the graphic organizers on a bulletin board.

Small Group ●●

Divide the class into pairs. Reproduce "Country Summer" and "Paulo's Birthday Pizza" on page 11 and its matching graphic organizer for each pair. One student should read the passage aloud to the other. Encourage the other student to listen closely. Then, the listener should fill in as much of the graphic organizer as possible. The listener should then pass the graphic organizer back to the reader. The reader should fill in any missing spaces without consulting the text. Have each pair switch roles and repeat the exercise with the second story.

Whole Class ●●●

Reproduce one of the graphic organizers on page 10 or 12 on a transparency. Read the corresponding story out loud to the class. Then, fill in the organizer as a class. Encourage all students to share their ideas.

Answer Key (suggested answers)

"Country Summer" (Page 9)

Main Idea: A girl helps out on her aunt and uncle's farm.

Details: Answers will vary.

"Paulo's Birthday Pizza" (Page 10)

Main Idea: Paulo makes his father a special gift for his birthday with the help of others.

Details: Answers will vary.

Country Summer

Last summer, I spent a month in the country. I stayed with Uncle Ray, Aunt Jane, and my cousin, Tim. I helped care for their animals.

I fed the chickens each morning. The first day, Aunt Jane handed me a bucket. It was filled with cracked corn. Then, she showed me where to go.

Those chickens were smart. They knew what was in the bucket. As soon as they spotted me, they came running.

After I fed the chickens, I collected eggs in a basket. I loved that job. It was a real treasure hunt.

Aunt Jane made pancakes for breakfast. We topped them with fresh butter and warm syrup. They were very good. Aunt Jane used my eggs to make them. That made them taste even better.

After breakfast, Tim and I took our scraps to Daisy, the pig. They were just leftover pancakes and bits of bacon. But Daisy thought they were a feast. She closed her eyes as she chewed. When she finished, she grunted her thanks.

Jasper was Tim's horse. Tim and I cleaned out his stall every afternoon. We brushed his brown coat and his long mane. We picked the dried mud away from his steel shoes. Then, we took turns riding him.

Tim and I helped my uncle milk the cow after dinner. The cow's name was Anna. The three of us walked across the yard together. The sun was going down. Tree frogs were starting to sing. There was something special about the quiet. We didn't talk.

Uncle Ray told me to pat Anna. He said to talk to her softly. At first, I didn't know what to say. Then, I thought about what might interest a cow.

I told her I liked her big brown eyes. Then, I talked about her neat stall in the cool, dark barn. I said she was lucky to live with Uncle Ray, Aunt Jane, and Tim.

Uncle Ray said I did a good job. He said that Anna liked me. Tim agreed. He said I was a natural.

I am going back to the farm next summer. I am looking forward to it. Tim says the animals really miss me. I know I miss them. Of course, I miss Uncle Ray, Aunt Jane, and Tim, too.

"Country Summer"
Graphic Organizer

Name:________________

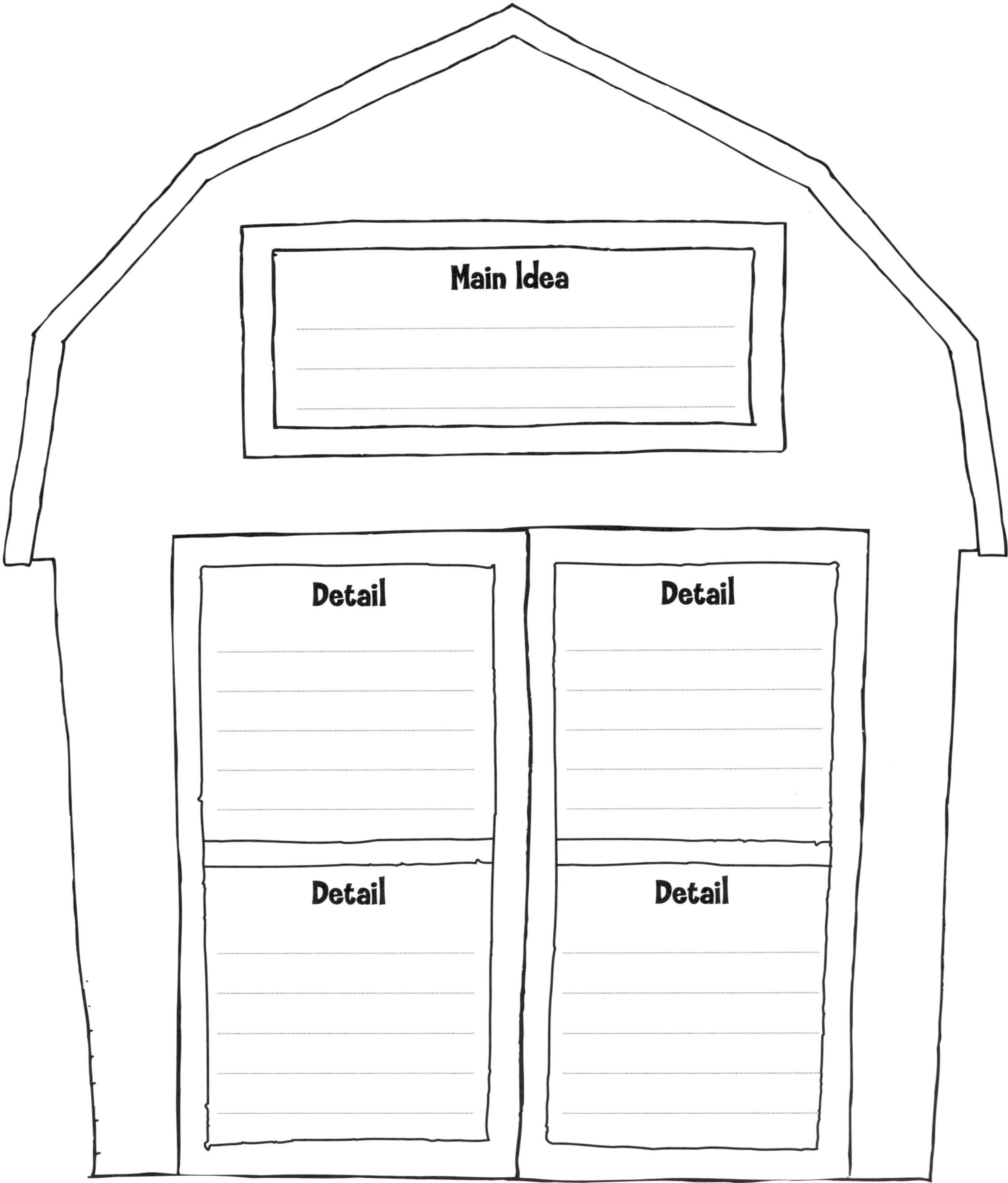

Paulo's Birthday Pizza

Paulo's father was having a birthday. Paulo wanted to give him a special gift. But his father did not need anything. If he wanted something, he just went to the store and bought it. Paulo had to think of something his father couldn't buy.

Paulo knew that pizza was his father's favorite food. Many shops in town sold pizza. Paulo's father had tried them all.

Paulo decided to make a pizza that was different. It would be the most special pizza ever. His father's birthday pizza would have only the best of everything.

Paulo bought a crust from Antonio. He had a small bakery on the corner. Antonio's crust was fresh, soft, and thick. Nobody made crust as good as Antonio's.

Paulo told Antonio why he wanted the crust. Antonio smiled. He gave Paulo a special box and wished his father a happy birthday. The box was big. Paulo carried it very carefully.

Then, Paulo walked down to Main Street. He bought a quart of sauce from Maria's Italian Grocery. Nobody made sauce as thick and spicy as Maria's. He told Maria why he wanted the sauce. She clapped her hands and gave Paulo a special bag. Then, she wished his father a happy birthday. The bag was heavy. Paulo did not want to drop it. He carried it very carefully.

Next, he bought a block of cheese from Aldo's Dairy. He told Aldo's sister, Carla, why he wanted the cheese. Carla nodded. She grated it for him. Then, she wished his father a happy birthday.

On his way home, Paulo stopped at Gino's vegetable stand. He bought two green peppers. He told Gino why he wanted the peppers. Gino used a big, sharp knife to slice them. Each pepper ring was perfect. Then, Gino wished Paulo's father a happy birthday.

Paulo carried his packages home. Then, he made the pizza. He spread out the crust and put the sauce, cheese, and peppers on it. Then, he put the pizza in the oven.

When Paulo brought his pizza to the table, his father said, "What's this?"

"It's a very special pizza. Take a bite and you will see."

His father smiled. He took a bite. "Amazing! I taste Antonio's crust, Maria's sauce, Aldo's cheese, and Gino's peppers."

"You are right," said Paulo. "They all wish you a happy birthday, and so do I."

Paulo's father gave him a hug. "This is the most special gift ever."

"Paulo's Birthday Pizza"
Graphic Organizer

Name:

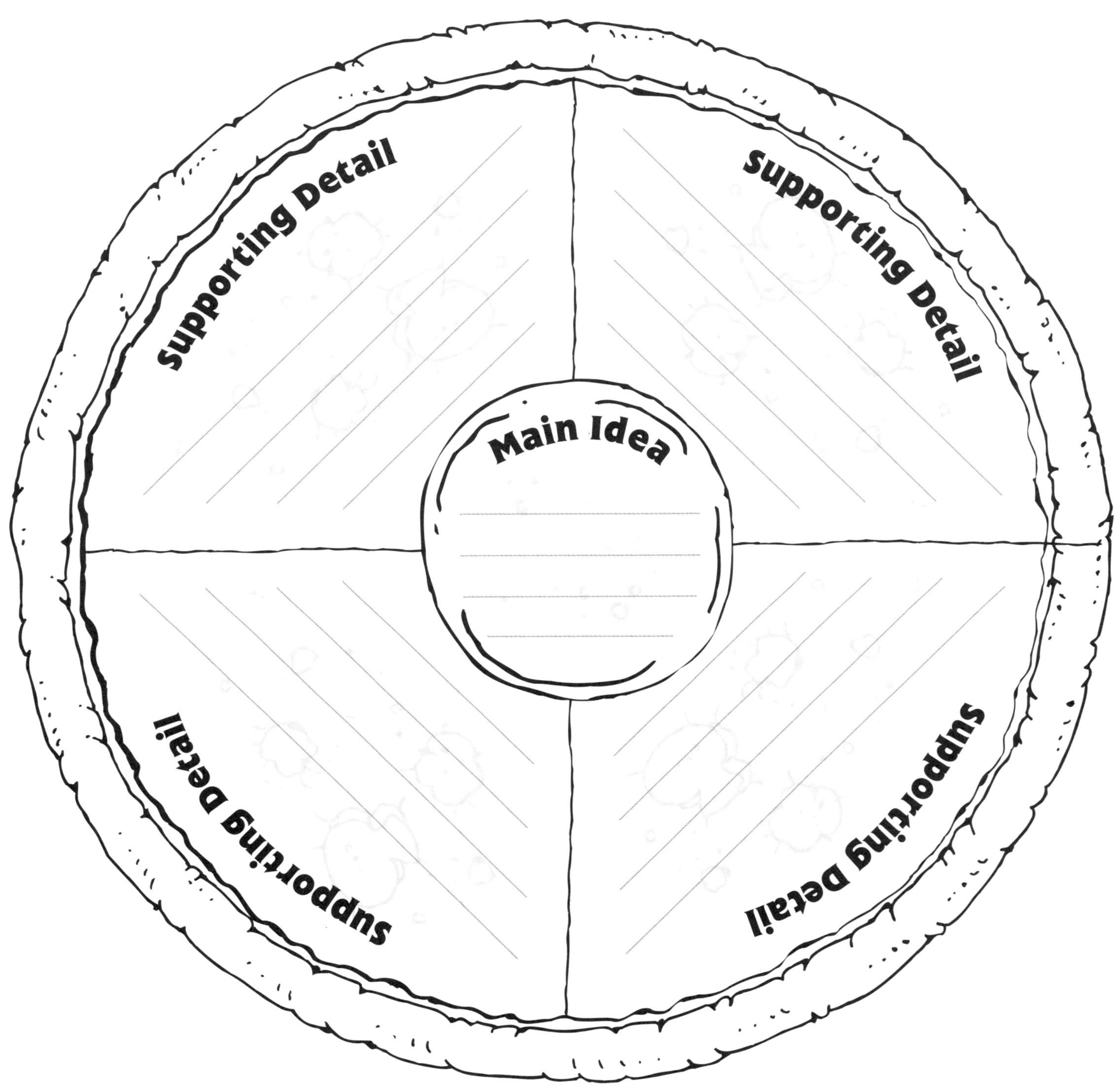

Directions: Comic Strips

Individual

Reproduce A Comic Strip Tale on page 14 and A Story in Pictures on page 15 for each student. (To save paper, make two-sided copies.) Encourage students to study the pictures. Then, have them fill in the blanks by writing sentences describing what they see in the pictures. Next, on separate sheets of paper, have students write appropriate titles for both sets of pictures and draw pictures for the covers. Explain that the title of the story should be the main idea, while the captions are the supporting details.

When all students have finished, discuss the activity as a class. Ask students to share their captions and titles.

Small Group

Divide students into groups of three or four. Reproduce Make Your Own Comic Strip for each group, as well as one of the picture sets. Invite group members to work together to draw their own comic strip. Encourage them to use the picture set as an example. Instruct them to write a caption under each picture and give their comic strips titles. Encourage groups to share their comic strips with the class. Then, hang them on a bulletin board for students to look at in their free time.

Whole Class

After completing the previous activity, invite members of each group to act out their comic strip for the rest of the class. Instruct other members of the class to write down the main idea of the comic strip after each performance. Hold a class discussion after each skit. Ask questions to elicit the main idea and supporting details. For example, to get the main idea, you might ask, "What was the story about?" For supporting details, you might ask, "What happened first?" or "What happened next?" or "What made you think that?"

A Comic Strip Tale

Name:

Directions: Write a caption beneath each picture to tell a story.

A Story in Pictures

Name:

Directions: Write a caption beneath each picture to tell a story.

Make Your Own Comic Strip

Name:______________________________

Directions: Science Outlines

Individual

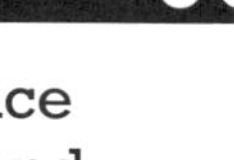

Reproduce "Frogs" on page 18 or "The Face of the Earth" on page 20 and its matching outline on page 19 or 21 for each student. Instruct students to read the text carefully, looking for the main idea and supporting details in each paragraph. Then, have students fill in the outline.

When all students have finished, display a transparency of the outline and discuss it as a class. As an extension, show a short, focused science film. After the viewing, help students create an outline. Show the film again. Discuss how making the outline helped them remember and understand the information.

Small Group

Divide the class into pairs. Reproduce "Frogs" or "The Face of the Earth" and its matching outline for each group. Have students take turns reading the passage aloud. Then, instruct students to complete the outline together.

Challenge each group to read a chapter from their science books and make an outline for the chapter.

Whole Class

Reproduce "Frogs" or "The Face of the Earth" and its matching outline for each student. Also, make copies on transparencies. Tell students to follow along as their classmates read the piece aloud. Allow students five minutes to fill in as much of the outline as they can. Then, display the transparency of the outline and complete it as a class activity.

Answer Key

"Frogs" Outline (Page 19)

1. amphibian a) eggs, water b) water, on land c) form d) blooded
2. cycle a) eggs, water b) eggs, tadpole c) tadpole, gills d) tadpole, legs, lungs a) frog, water
3. frogs, different a) tree b) water c) underground
4. sizes a) one foot b) one half-inch c) eight inches d) one inch
5. People a) insects, diseases, crops b) polluted water

"The Face of the Earth" Outline (Page 21)

1. Earth, smooth a) valleys, lakes, islands b) Maps
2. mountain a) mountains, range b) Rocky Mountains, mountain range c) Rockies, Canada, Mexico
3. world, oceans a) Earth, blue, oceans b) Pacific, world c) Atlantic, second d) oceans, connected
4. parts, ocean a) land, around b) Mediterranean, example
5. rivers, map, a) important b) Mississippi River, travel, business
6. feature, Earth a) large, flat b) wheat, corn, crops
7. world, freshwater a) Finland, lakes b) Baikal, oldest c) United States, Superior
8. planet a) water b) Hawaii, group, islands c) Greenland

Frogs

A frog is an amphibian. All amphibians have certain things in common. Like other amphibians, frogs lay their eggs in water. They spend the first part of their lives in the water. Then, they metamorphose, or change form. After that, they can live on land. Frogs are cold-blooded like other amphibians. Their body temperature matches the temperature around them. That is why some frogs like to sit on sunny rocks to keep warm.

Frogs have an interesting life cycle. Mother frogs lay their eggs in water. The water can be a lake. It can be a quiet pool in a stream. It can even be a puddle. A special jelly protects her eggs. When the eggs hatch, a tadpole is born. Tadpoles are sometimes called pollywogs. The tadpole looks like a little fish. It has a tail, and it breathes through gills. Tadpoles cannot leave the water. They cannot breathe air, and they do not have legs.

The tadpole eats and eats. It grows and grows. Bullfrog tadpoles can live in ponds for up to three years before they change into frogs. Spadefoot toad tadpoles can change in just 12 days. Eventually, all tadpoles grow legs. They also develop lungs. Then, one day, new little frogs or toads hop out of the water.

Different kinds of frogs live in different places. Spring peepers are tree frogs. They live in eastern forests. Leopard frogs live near streams or ponds. They are very shy. When enemies come near, these spotted frogs dive into the water. Leopard frogs are common in the United States and Canada. Spadefoot toads are also common in the United States. They live in places that are hot and dry in the summer. They dig burrows. These underground homes keep their skin from drying out.

Frogs come in many different sizes. Goliath frogs are the largest in the world. They can be up to one foot long. The world's smallest frogs live in Cuban rain forests. They are less than one half-inch long. Bullfrogs are the largest frogs in the United States and Canada. They can be up to eight inches long. The chorus frogs that sing in eastern meadows are less than one inch long.

People need frogs. These little creatures eat lots of insects. Insects can carry diseases and harm crops. Frogs can also help keep us safe. They breathe though their skin. This makes them very sensitive to polluted water. When rivers or lakes contain poisons, frogs get sick. When frogs are dying, scientists pay attention. It could mean that the water is unsafe for people, too.

"Frogs" Outline

Name: ____________________

1 A frog is an ____________.

a A frog lays her ____________ in ____________.

b A frog spends part of its life in ____________ and part of its life ____________.

c A frog metamorphoses, or changes ____________.

d A frog is cold-____________.

2 Frogs have an interesting life ____________.

a Female frogs lay their ____________ in ____________.

b The ____________ hatch, and a ____________ is born.

c The ____________ breathes through ____________ like a fish.

d The ____________ grows ____________ and develops ____________.

e The little ____________ hops out of the ____________.

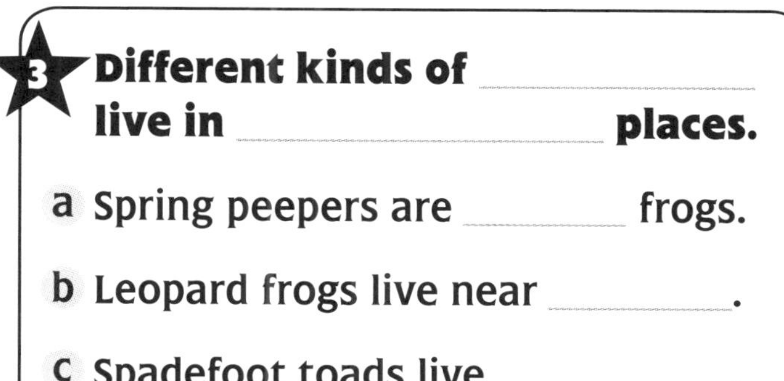

3 Different kinds of ____________ live in ____________ places.

a Spring peepers are ____________ frogs.

b Leopard frogs live near ____________.

c Spadefoot toads live ____________.

4 Frogs come in many different ____________.

a The largest frog in the world can be ____________ long.

b The smallest frogs in the world are less than ____________ long.

c The bullfrog can be up to ____________ long.

d Chorus frogs are less than ____________ long.

5 ____________ need frogs.

a Frogs eat ____________ that can carry ____________ and harm ____________.

b Frogs are very sensitive to ____________ ____________.

The Face of the Earth

The Earth is not smooth and flat. It has mountains, valleys, lakes, and islands. Relief maps show these features.

The world has many mountain groups. A group of mountains is called a range. The Rocky Mountains are a large mountain range. The Rockies stretch from Canada into New Mexico.

The world also has some large oceans. Earth is sometimes called "the blue planet." This is because of the oceans. The Pacific Ocean is the largest ocean in the world. The Atlantic Ocean is the second largest. However, the oceans are all connected.

Seas are smaller parts of the ocean. They usually have land around them. The Mediterranean is a good example of a sea.

Even big rivers are easy to spot on a world map. They are important to the people who live near them. The Mississippi River is used for travel and business.

Plains are another feature of the Earth. Plains are large, flat lands. Farmers on the plains grow wheat, corn, and other crops.

The world has many freshwater lakes. In fact, Finland alone has 187,888 of them! Lake Baikal in Russia is the oldest lake in the world. The largest lake in the United States is Lake Superior.

Islands are also features of our planet. An island is a piece of land with water all around it. The state of Hawaii is a group of islands. Greenland is another very large island.

The surface of our Earth has many features. It has high points and low points. It has flat areas, too. It has oceans, rivers, and lakes. It has land surrounded by water. It has water surrounded by land. Each part of the world is interesting and important.

"The Face of the Earth" Outline

Name: ____________

1 The ____________ is not ____________ and flat.

a It has mountains, ____________, ____________, and ____________.

b ____________ show these features.

2 The world has many ____________ groups.

a A group of ____________ is called a ____________.

b The ____________ ____________ are a large ____________ ____________.

c The ____________ stretch from ____________ into ____________.

3 The ____________ also has some large ____________.

a The ____________ is called "the ____________ planet" because of the ____________.

b The ____________ is the largest ocean in the ____________.

c The ____________ is the ____________ largest.

d The ____________ are ____________.

4 Seas are smaller ____________ of the ____________.

a Seas usually have ____________ ____________ them.

b The ____________ is a good ____________ of a sea.

5 Big ____________ are easy to spot on a ____________.

a Big rivers are ____________ to people.

b The ____________ is used for ____________ and ____________.

6 Plains are another ____________ on the face of the ____________.

a Plains are ____________, ____________ lands.

b Farmers on the plains grow ____________, ____________, and other ____________.

7 The ____________ has many ____________ lakes.

a ____________ has 187,888 ____________.

b Lake ____________ in Russia is the ____________ lake in the world.

c The largest lake in the ____________ ____________ is Lake ____________.

8 Islands are also features of our ____________.

a An island is a piece of land with ____________ all around it.

b The state of ____________ is a ____________ of ____________.

c ____________ is a very large island.

Directions: Main Ideas about Places

Individual

Reproduce Main Ideas at School on page 23 and Main Ideas in the Mountains on page 24 for each student. Instruct students to carefully read each paragraph and select the correct main idea from the choices provided.

When all students are finished, display one or both of the pages on a transparency, and discuss the answers as a class. As an extension, encourage students to name the main ideas in paragraphs they read as part of their social studies or science lessons.

Small Group

Divide students into groups of three or four. Reproduce "Main Ideas at School" and "Main Ideas in the Mountains" for each group. Have each student in the group read a paragraph aloud and then use the accompanying multiple-choice question to quiz other group members.

When all groups are finished, go over the answers as a class. Did all students answer the same way?

Whole Class

Reproduce "Main Ideas at School" or "Main Ideas in the Mountains," covering up the multiple-choice answers, on a transparency. Write the main idea for each paragraph, out of order, on the board or on a separate transparency. Assign each main idea a letter. Have students match each paragraph to the correct main idea, writing their answers on blank paper. Then, ask for a show of hands to see how many students chose each answer. Record the results on the board. Encourage the class to discuss the results, and allow students a chance to change their minds. Then, reveal the correct answers and discuss them as a class.

Answer Key

Main Ideas at School (Page 23)

1 b
2. a
3. c
4. b

Main Ideas in the Mountains (Page 24)

1. b
2. c
3. a
4. b

Main Ideas at School

Name:

Directions: Circle the main idea after reading each paragraph.

Paragraph 1

Teachers work with students in classrooms. Many schools have classroom aides, too. School office workers answer questions. They also order supplies. The nurse helps to keep students healthy. The counselor makes sure they get support. Cafeteria workers serve good, hot food. The custodian keeps the building in working order. The principal is in charge of the staff. She helps everyone work together to serve student needs. There are many kinds of jobs at a school.

a) Teachers work with students in classrooms.

b) There are many kinds of jobs at a school.

c) The principal is in charge of the staff.

Paragraph 2

Some schools have grassy yards. Others have paved playgrounds. Some schools have auditoriums and gyms. Others have multipurpose rooms. Schools are the same in some ways and different in others. Some schools have just one big building. Others have many small buildings. Some schools are old. Others are new. All schools are places where students learn.

a) Schools are the same in some ways and different in others.

b) All schools are places where students learn.

c) Some schools have just one big building.

Paragraph 3

Students study many subjects in school. They learn to read. They also learn to write. They study math. In social studies, students learn how people work together. In science, they study the natural world. Art helps students to think in new ways. Music helps them find patterns. Gym class helps them stay active.

a) In social studies, students learn how people work together.

b) Art helps students to think in new ways.

c) Students study many subjects in school.

Paragraph 4

Preschools help children get ready for school. Grade schools teach basic skills. Middle schools teach teens to study and think. High schools help students get ready to live on their own. Colleges help students become leaders. Different schools serve different needs.

a) Preschools help children get ready for school.

b) Different schools serve different needs.

c) Middle schools teach teens to study and think.

Main Ideas in the Mountains

Name: ______________________

Directions: Circle the main idea after reading each paragraph.

Paragraph 1

A beam of sunlight hits the forest floor. It helps a little bush grow. The leaves of the bush are green and tender. A grasshopper lands on the bush. It eats some of the leaves. Along hops a frog. It snaps up the grasshopper. A snake slithers along the stream bank. It swallows the frog. That night, an owl swoops down from its treetop nest. It catches the snake. It is easy to find a chain of life in the woods.

a) A bush grows on the forest floor.

b) It is easy to find a chain of life in the woods.

c) A grasshopper eats some of the leaves.

Paragraph 2

Camping in the mountains is fun. During the day, campers hike shady trails. They canoe on clear lakes. They catch fresh fish. At night, campers cook dinner over crackling fires. They enjoy the sparkling stars. Then, they slip into warm sleeping bags. They hear wind in the trees. They listen to owls calling in the dark. Campers fall asleep smiling.

a) At night, campers cook dinner over crackling fires.

b) During the day, campers hike shady trails.

c) Camping in the mountains is fun.

Paragraph 3

It is a warm day in late spring. Sunlight hits a patch of snow on the mountain-side. Some of the snow melts. The water drips down. It meets up with trickles from other melting snow. The icy water forms a small stream. It races down the hill. It carries dirt and pebbles downhill. It digs a shallow bed on the hillside. The little stream meets another. It flows faster. The bigger stream carries more dirt and bigger rocks. It runs into a river. Other streams join the river, too. The roaring river eats away at its banks. Pushed by the fast water, rocks dig out the river's bed. Running water is cutting a canyon.

a) Running water is cutting a canyon.

b) It is a warm day in late spring.

c) The bigger stream carries more dirt and larger rocks out of its bed.

Paragraph 4

Forest rangers have many jobs. They watch for insects and diseases that can kill trees. Rangers protect animals from hunters who do not obey the rules. They spot fires and help to put them out. Forest rangers take care of campgrounds. Sometimes, they find lost hikers. They measure the flow of streams. Rangers enjoy teaching visitors to love the land.

a) Rangers protect animals from hunters who do not obey the rules.

b) Forest rangers have many jobs.

c) Forest rangers take care of campgrounds.

Directions: Which Detail Doesn't Belong?

Individual ●

Reproduce Favorite Places on page 26 or Home on page 27 for each student. Instruct students to read each passage carefully and underline the sentence that doesn't belong in each paragraph.

When all students are finished, invite them to share their answers with the class. Discuss why the underlined sentences do not support the main idea of the paragraph.

Small Group ●●

Have each student write an original paragraph, including one sentence that does not support the main idea. Review paragraphs for main ideas and extra details. Then, divide the class into pairs. Tell the partners to exchange paragraphs.

Challenge each student to find the sentence that doesn't belong in the paragraph and underline it, then write down the main idea of the paragraph.

When both partners have finished, have them discuss their answers with each other.

Whole Class 

Reproduce "Favorite Places" or "Home" on a transparency. Divide the class into two teams. Show one paragraph at a time on the overhead. The first team to tap the edge of their desks and state the sentence that doesn't belong earns a point. Award bonus points for correct explanations. The team with the most points at the end of the game wins.

Answer Key

Favorite Places (Page 26)

1. Science is an interesting subject.
2. Many frogs live near ponds.
3. The bank is next to the library.
4. My mom goes to the store every Monday.

Home (Page 27)

1. We have a dog named Toby.
2. Guitars are stringed instruments.
3. We have a pool out back.
4. The Tyrannosaurus Rex was a meat-eating dinosaur.

Favorite Places

Name:

Directions: Underline the sentence that doesn't belong in each paragraph.

Paragraph 1

Blue Lake Park is a great place to spend a weekend afternoon. Some people like to ride their bikes. There is a special trail for them. It goes around the lake. Other people rent horses. They ride up in the hills. Science is an interesting subject. Families with little children head for the zoo or the playground. In the summer, local teams use the baseball diamond. Their friends sit in the stands and cheer them on.

Paragraph 2

It is fun to visit Sundown Beach in the summer. Many frogs live near ponds. Some beach visitors surf. Others explore tide pools or collect shells. Many build sand castles or wade in the ocean. Fishermen spend all day on the nearby pier. They drop their lines into the water and wait for fish to bite. Kite fliers like the sand. They hold their kites up and wait for the wind. Then, they lie back and watch. All they have to do is let out more string. The kites soar high above the beach.

Paragraph 3

The public library is my favorite place. I love to go there on hot afternoons. The building is always quiet and cool. The bank is next to the library. In the library, the rules are simple. If I follow them, nobody will tell me what to do. The library has so many wonderful books. I can pick out any one I want. When I open a library book, I can go anywhere. I can even visit another planet. I can be a famous athlete or a movie star. In the library, I am free.

Paragraph 4

Dry leaves on the cottonwood tree rattle. Cars leave clouds of dust behind. Birds search for a drop of water. My mom goes to the store every Monday. Suddenly, dark clouds roll in. Lightning flashes. Thunder rumbles. Sheets of rain sweep across the hot streets. Then, little pellets of hail pound on our roof. It is like sitting inside a drum. It is so exciting! Then, just as suddenly, the sun comes out. The last of the clouds drift away. Birds take baths in the puddles. Other creatures come out to drink. I love afternoon showers in the summer.

Home

Name:____________________

Directions: Underline the sentence that doesn't belong in each paragraph.

Paragraph 1

Our kitchen is really a family room. We all enjoy eating at the kitchen table. Everybody meets there for breakfast. My dad and brothers laugh and talk while they wash the dishes. Before leaving for school, each of us checks the calendar on the refrigerator door. After school, I sit on a kitchen stool and chat with Mom. We have a dog named Toby. At dinner time, we sit down at the table again. We share all the great things that happened. We share the bad things, too. At our kitchen table, everything seems better.

Paragraph 2

Friends visit us often. They love our living room. Some sit on the couch. Others snuggle into our comfortable chairs. We have a soft, thick carpet, so I sit on the floor. There is a stereo in the living room. Sometimes we listen to music. Guitars are stringed instruments. Other times, we eat popcorn and watch TV. There is a folding table in the corner. When we want to play board games, we set it up. Our living room is a great place to have fun with friends.

Paragraph 3

I used to share a room with my brother. Last week we moved to a bigger house across the street. Now, I have a room of my own. It's great! My window overlooks the sidewalk. I can see my friends coming before they knock on the door. I have my own desk and a bookcase. My dad built me a chest for my toys and games. We have a pool out back. Mom let me choose a new bedspread. It has pictures of superheroes on it. My new bedroom has everything I want.

Paragraph 4

The study is downstairs. It is next to the living room. There are bookcases on two of the walls. I can't reach the books at the top. But the books I need are on the bottom shelves. The Tyrannosaurus Rex was a meat-eating dinosaur. One of the study walls has a big window. Most of the time, the drapes are closed. When they are open, you can see a fountain in the garden. The computer is on a big desk across from the window. There are cozy chairs. Our study is a pleasant place to talk, read, and think.

Directions: Scrambled Ideas

Individual

Reproduce "Jake Gets a Dog" on page 29 or "Taking Care of Woofer" on page 31 for each student. Tell students the paragraphs are scrambled, and they must put the sentences in the correct order. Have them use the lines below the paragraph to rewrite the paragraph correctly. Then, tell them to write down the main idea of the paragraph.

When all students have finished, display transparencies of each paragraph, and discuss the activity as a class. What clues did students use to put the sentences in the correct order? Encourage students to share their main idea sentences.

Next, make sets of the Scrambled Idea cards on pages 30 and 32, and place them in a learning center. Challenge students to put them in the correct order. For a cross-curricular approach, write down step-by-step directions on index cards for an art or science project your class is working on. Place them in the learning center. Challenge students to put them in the correct order and state the main idea. Then, challenge them to make the art or science project. Evaluate them on their ability to sequence, find the main idea, and follow directions.

As an extension, challenge students to write step-by-step instructions for making lemonade or a peanut butter and jelly sandwich. Have students share their instructions with the rest of the class. Are any steps missing? How do they know?

Small Group

Divide the class into groups of three or four. Reproduce Scrambled Ideas 1 on page 30 for each group. When all groups are ready, say "Go!" The first student has 30 seconds to figure out what the first sentence of the paragraph should be and mark it with "#1." He or she then passes the worksheet to the next student, who has 30 seconds to figure out the second sentence. Continue until all sentences have been numbered. The team to finish first with their sentences correctly numbered wins. Repeat the exercise with Scrambled Ideas 2 on page 32.

Whole Class

Reproduce one set each of the Scrambled Idea cards, and cut them apart. Put the first set in a bag. Divide the class into two teams. Have the first team come to the front of the room, pull the sentences out of the bag, and put them in the right order.

When Team One is finished, Team Two decides whether the sentence order is correct. If it is not, members of Team Two must rearrange the sentences correctly. Teams alternate until the sentences are correct. Repeat the exercise with the second set of cards.

Or, reproduce two sets of the same cards, cut them apart, and put each set in a separate bag. Give a bag to each team. Have both teams attempt to put their sentences in order as quickly as possible. The team to correctly finish first is the winner.

Jake Gets a Dog

Name:

Jake looked into Woofer's big brown eyes. His mother said he could pick just one. Jake begged her for more. Jake's mother paid Woofer's fees. Jake attached a leash to the little beagle's collar. Jake saw a lot of cute dogs at the shelter. Jake led his puppy to the car. Finally, Jake picked up a beagle puppy named Woofer. Then, his mother drove them home. His mother would not change her mind. Jake's mother said he could have a dog. At that moment, he knew Woofer was the one. She drove Jake to the animal shelter. He wanted to take all of them home.

The main idea is:

Scrambled Card Set 1

At that moment, he knew Woofer was the one.

Jake attached a leash to the little beagle's collar.

Jake's mother paid Woofer's fees.

Finally, Jake picked up a beagle puppy named Woofer.

His mother would not change her mind.

She drove Jake to the animal shelter.

He wanted to take all of them home.

Jake begged her for more.

His mother said he could pick just one.

Jake saw a lot of cute dogs at the shelter.

Jake led his puppy to the car.

Jake's mother said he could have a dog.

Then, his mother drove them home.

Jake looked into Woofer's big brown eyes.

Taking Care of Woofer

Name:

Then, Jake gave his dog a biscuit. Jake stepped into his jeans. Jake let the dog out into the fenced yard. "Good boy!" he said. Jake followed him. When Woofer came back, Jake rubbed his ears. It was his dog whining. Woofer wanted to go outside. He slipped on his shoes. When Jake woke up, he heard a sad sound. On the way out of his bedroom, Jake grabbed a T-shirt. Taking care of Woofer was hard sometimes, but Jake loved doing it. Tail wagging, Woofer waited for him by the back door. He pulled it over his head and walked down the hall. Then, he pulled on some socks. Woofer bounded down the stairs.

The main idea is:

Scrambled Card Set 2

"Good boy!" he said.

Taking care of Woofer was hard sometimes, but Jake loved doing it.

Jake let the dog out into the fenced yard.

It was his dog whining.

On the way out of his bedroom, Jake grabbed a T-shirt.

He pulled it over his head and walked down the hall.

Then, he pulled on some socks.

Woofer wanted to go outside.

Jake followed him.

Woofer bounded down the stairs.

Jake stepped into his jeans.

He slipped on his shoes.

When Woofer came back, Jake rubbed his ears.

Tail wagging, Woofer waited for him by the back door.

Then, Jake gave his dog a biscuit.

When Jake woke up, he heard a sad sound.

Directions: Sentence Match

Individual ●

Reproduce Ideas with Support 1 and 2 on pages 34 and 35 for each student. Cut the cards apart, label the back of each card "main idea" or "supporting," and number each pair. Working with the cards faceup, challenge students to identify the main idea sentences and supporting sentences. Have them match each supporting detail to its main idea sentence. Tell them to flip the cards over to check their accuracy. When all students are finished, discuss the activity as a class.

Small Group ●●

Divide the class into groups of three or four students. Reproduce one set of Ideas with Support per group. Challenge groups to be the first to correctly match each main idea sentence with its supporting detail. When the first group is finished, have the students share their matches with the class. They should tell whether each is a supporting sentence or main idea sentence. Invite class members to agree or disagree. Encourage them to discuss their reasoning. If the first group has any incorrect matches, let the remaining groups have another chance. The first group to finish correctly is the winner.

Answer Key

Ideas with Support 1 (Page 34)

Main Idea: There are 23 students in our class. **Supporting Detail:** There are 12 boys and 11 girls.

MI: My room is a mess.
SD: There are books and toys all over the floor.

MI: I have been reading all summer. **SD:** The first book I read was *Ramona the Pest* by Beverly Cleary.

MI: My sister and I cooked dinner last night.
SD: I made the salad.

MI: There are many kinds of turtles.
SD: Tortoises are turtles that live on land.

MI: Some interesting mammals live in the ocean.
SD: Whales are warm-blooded and breath air.

MI: All birds have some things in common.
SD: They lay eggs.

MI: Our town has two high schools.
SD: East High School is near the main highway.

Ideas with Support 2 (Page 35)

Main Idea: I found four different insects in our backyard. **Supporting Detail:** The first one was a swallowtail butterfly.

MI: I earn my allowance by doing chores.
SD: I take out the trash every afternoon.

MI: Goldfish are good pets for an apartment.
SD: They never bark or howl.

MI: It is important to follow bike safety rules.
SD: Always wear a helmet.

MI: Our school has three third-grade classes.
SD: Mrs. Davis has been teaching third grade for two years.

MI: Some animals eat plants.
SD: Deer love grass and leaves.

MI: A landscape is a picture of a place.
SD: Mountain scenes are peaceful.

MI: My mom and I planted a garden last month.
SD: Our squash plants are already starting to sprout.

Ideas with Support 1

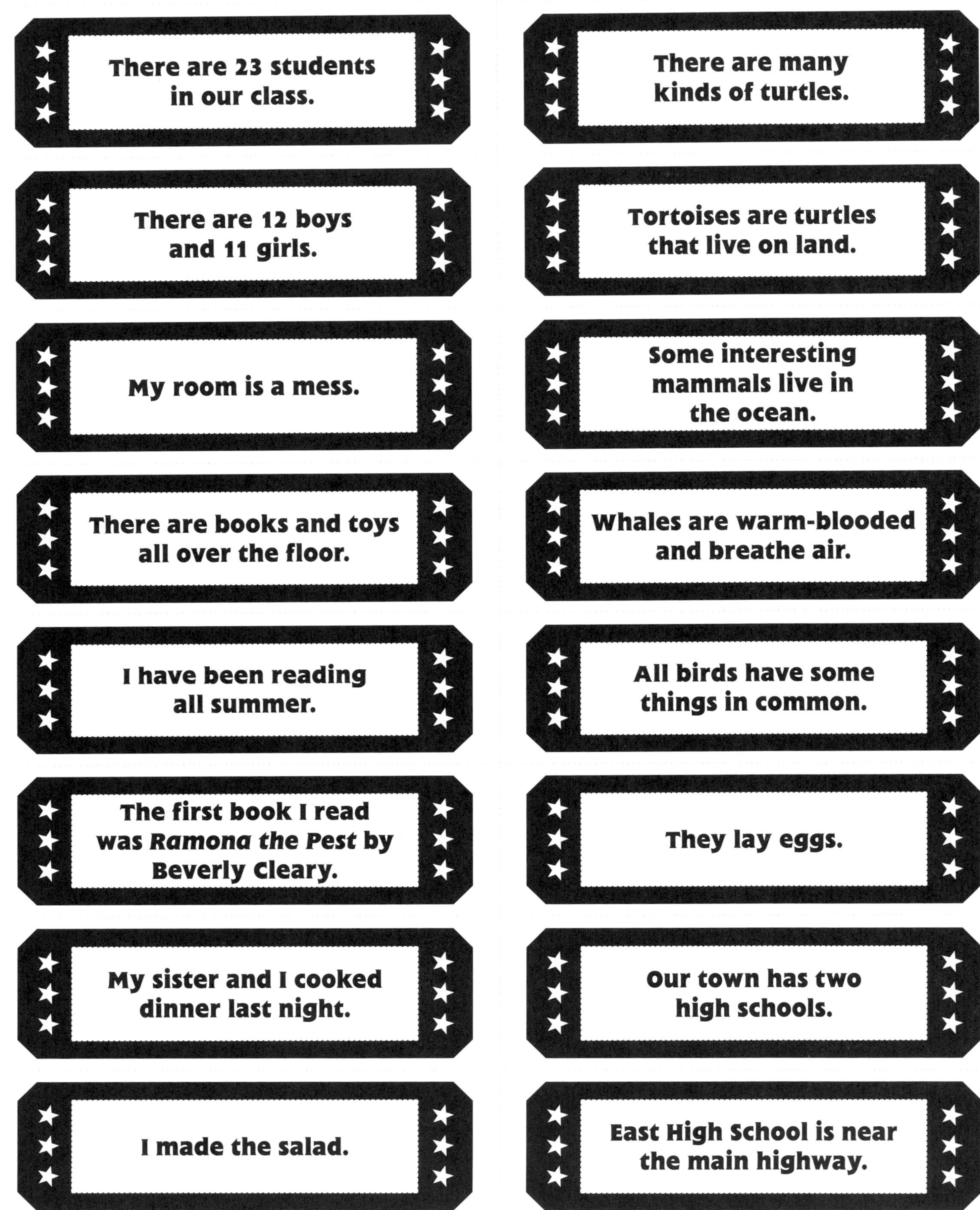

Ideas with Support 2

Directions: Matching Main Ideas

Individual

Reproduce one Missing Main Ideas worksheet on page 37 or 38 for each student. Tell students that each paragraph is missing a main idea sentence. Challenge them to write a main idea sentence for each paragraph.

When all students are finished, invite them to share their main ideas with the rest of the class. Write them on the board or a transparency as students read them. How alike or different are students' main ideas? Compare them to the main ideas provided below.

Small Group

Divide the class into groups of three or four. Reproduce one Missing Paragraphs worksheet on page 39 or 40 for each group. Have each student choose a different main idea sentence from the list. Have students write paragraphs based on their main idea sentences. Then, invite students to read their paragraphs to each other. They should then discuss whether or not the supporting details match the main idea.

Whole Class

Reproduce the Missing Main Ideas pages on transparencies and the Missing Paragraph pages on heavy paper. Cut the main idea sentences out, and place the circles in bags, keeping the two sets separate. Divide the class into two teams. Display one sheet of paragraphs on the transparency. Invite a player from each team to draw a sentence out of the matching bag. The player who correctly matches his or her main idea sentence to a paragraph first wins a point for his or her team. Reward the team with the most points at the end of each round.

Answer Key (suggested answers)

Missing Main Ideas 1 (Page 37)

1. There are several stages in the life cycle of a moth.
2. Wild animals have different kinds of homes.
3. Baby animals have different names.
4. I can close my eyes and see my room.
5. My school is an interesting place.
6. I caught a terrible cold.
7. The music teacher wants me to choose an instrument.

Missing Main Ideas 2 (Page 38)

1. Mom and I went to the store to buy food for dinner.
2. My first swimming lesson was almost my last.
3. This is what I saw at the parade.
4. Saturday was a great day.
5. Each of the four seasons is special.
6. Last weekend, we went to the big shoe store in the mall.
7. My favorite store is a unique place.

Missing Main Ideas 1

Paragraph 1

Tiny eggs hatch in the warm spring sun. Little caterpillars crawl out and start to eat. They grow bigger and bigger. Finally, the caterpillars spin cocoons. Inside their cocoons, the caterpillars are changing. One day, the cocoons open. Moths fly out.

Paragraph 2

Ants live in colonies underground. Bees build hives out of wax. Owls make nests in hollow trees. Beavers build lodges. Foxes live in dens, and mountain lions live in caves.

Paragraph 3

A baby bear is called a cub. A kit is a baby fox. A baby penguin is called a chick. A baby bison is a calf, and so is a baby whale. A baby wolf is called a pup. A baby duck is a duckling and a baby goose is a gosling.

Paragraph 4

My bed has a red and white striped quilt. My curtains have red and white stripes, too. My dresser is painted white. It has three drawers. My closet door has a long mirror on it. I check my clothes and my hair in the mirror before I leave for school. I have a collection of stuffed animals. I keep them in a bookcase under the window.

Paragraph 5

The main building is two stories high. It is made of red brick. A sign over the door reads 1925. That is when the school was built. The multipurpose room and the cafeteria are on the first floor. The first- and second-grade classes are on the first floor, too. Third- and fourth-graders climb concrete stairs to the second floor. There are portable classrooms near the playground for the fifth-graders. Preschool and kindergarten classes meet in a separate building.

Paragraph 6

When I woke up on Tuesday, my head was pounding. I tried to get up and get dressed, but I was too dizzy. Mom took my temperature. She said I was too sick to go to school. She told me to stay in bed and get some extra sleep. She brought me some juice and set up my favorite movie on the DVD player. On Wednesday, I started sneezing and I couldn't stop.

Paragraph 7

The flute has a cheerful sound. It is like a bird. The cello has a rich, deep voice. The trumpet is exciting. It makes me think of parades. I like them all, but I want to play the drums. They make my heart pound!

Missing Main Ideas 2

Name:

Paragraph 1

First, we went to the produce department. Mom chose a head of lettuce and some tomatoes. Then, we stopped by the meat counter. The butcher measured out a pound of ground beef for meatballs. We picked up a pound of cheese in the deli department. Then, we grabbed a box of pasta and a jar of sauce. We were ready to check out.

Paragraph 2

The teacher told us to put our faces in the water. She said to blow bubbles. It sounded like fun, but it wasn't. The chlorine in the water burned my eyes. Once, I breathed in before I lifted my face up. I coughed. It was hard to breathe for awhile. On the way home, I told my dad I didn't want to learn to swim after all. He just smiled and said to try one more lesson.

Paragraph 3

First, the drill team marched by. They were twirling long blue-and-white flags. The cloth made a whirring sound as it whipped through the air. The high school band came next. They were playing a famous march. There were two rows of trumpets and a row of tubas. They flashed like gold in the morning sun. After the band, a white car with the top down went past. The winner of the Miss Bensonville contest was sitting on top of the back seat. She was wearing a white dress and a crown. She waved to everyone.

Paragraph 4

We all woke up late, even Dad. Mom made pancakes. We ate them with fresh strawberries and real whipped cream. After breakfast, Dad drove us to the park. We walked around the lake. Denny, my little brother, chased a squirrel until the poor thing ran up a tree. Mom spread a blanket on the grass. She and Denny read a book while Dad and I played catch. Later, all of us watched a movie on TV. It was fun.

Paragraph 5

In the spring, days and nights are equal. Flowers bloom, and birds raise their families. In the summer, days are long, and nights are short. The weather is hot. In the fall, days and nights are equal again. Leaves turn red and gold. The first snow falls in the mountains. In the winter, nights are longer than days. The weather is cold. In some places, snow blankets the ground. It is very quiet. Bears and other animals curl up in their caves. The whole world seems to be waiting.

Paragraph 6

I tried on three pairs of sneakers. The first pair was much too small. They pinched my toes. The second pair fit, but I didn't like the color. The third pair was perfect, so we bought them. I am planning to wear them to school on Monday.

Paragraph 7

Along the side walls there are bins. They are filled with special stones. There are shells from ancient seas, and there are even flat prints of fish. There are silvery blocks of lead ore and brassy blocks of fool's gold. There are spiky crystals of quartz and purple amethyst. In the back of the shop are strings of beads made of stone. There are also little frogs, dragons, and fish carved from polished rock.

Name:

MAIN IDEA

There are several stages in the life cycle of a moth.

MAIN IDEA

Wild animals have different kinds of homes.

MAIN IDEA

Baby animals have different names.

MAIN IDEA

I can close my eyes and see my room.

MAIN IDEA

My school is an interesting place.

MAIN IDEA

I caught a terrible cold.

MAIN IDEA

The music teacher wants me to choose an instrument.

Name:

MAIN IDEA

My favorite store is a unique place.

MAIN IDEA

Saturday was a great day.

MAIN IDEA

Each of the four seasons is special.

MAIN IDEA

Mom and I went to the store to buy food for dinner.

MAIN IDEA

This is what I saw at the parade.

MAIN IDEA

Last weekend, we went to the big shoe store in the mall.

MAIN IDEA

My first swimming lesson was almost my last.

Directions: Thesis Statements

Individual ●

Reproduce Topic List 1 on page 42, cut the topics apart, and place them in a bag. Give each student a copy of the Bright Ideas Graphic Organizer on page 44. Explain to students that a thesis statement is a sentence that states the main idea of an essay or report, and that each paragraph in the essay must include details to support the thesis statement. Have each student draw a topic out of the bag and write a thesis statement and supporting details on the graphic organizer based on it. Circulate among students to help them form ideas. Invite students to share their graphic organizers with the class.

Small Group ●●

Separate the class into small groups. Reproduce The Idea Factory Graphic Organizer on page 45 for each group. Reproduce Topic List 2 on page 43, cut the topics apart, and place them in a bag. Have each group pull a topic out of the bag. Encourage students to work together to fill in the graphic organizer. First, have the students write down the topic, then fill in the "Ideas" section with facts they already know about the topic. They should use these ideas to write a working thesis statement. (For example, if the topic is "turtles," the students might write "Turtles live in freshwater" as their thesis statement.) Then, provide resources (such as library books or Internet access) for the students to research the topic further to make the thesis statement more specific. (For example, "Turtles live in freshwater ponds, lakes, and rivers.") When groups have completed the activity, invite them to share their graphic organizers with the rest of the class.

Whole Class

Reproduce Topic List 1 and 2, cut the topics apart, and place them in a bag. Divide the class into two teams. Have students from each team take turns drawing two topics out of the bag. Challenge them to combine the two topics into one "silly sentence" thesis statement. Have each team member read his or her silly sentence aloud. As an extension, have students write a "silly paragraph" based on the thesis statement. Award points for creativity and following directions. The team with the most points at the end wins.

Topic List 1

lizards	**a favorite book**	**exercise**
a party to remember	**rabbits**	**a fun game**
a favorite food	**pets**	**a favorite sport**
giraffes	**the sun**	**a favorite subject in school**
the seasons	**a favorite month**	**school**
a favorite day of the week	**a food chain**	**a vacation**
ducks	**healthy snacks**	**turtles**
bees	**desert plants**	**pumpkins**
Africa	**the library**	**Thanksgiving**

Topic List 2

snakes	bats	my best friend
grasshoppers	ladybugs	a holiday
family rules	class rules	an exciting ride
ants	seahorses	an interesting place in town
rain clouds	saving water	a favorite toy
nonliving things	living things	a favorite movie
magnets	a school fair	a favorite game
a school club	a chore at home	swimming
making a sandwich	gardens	butterflies

Bright Ideas Graphic Organizer

Name:

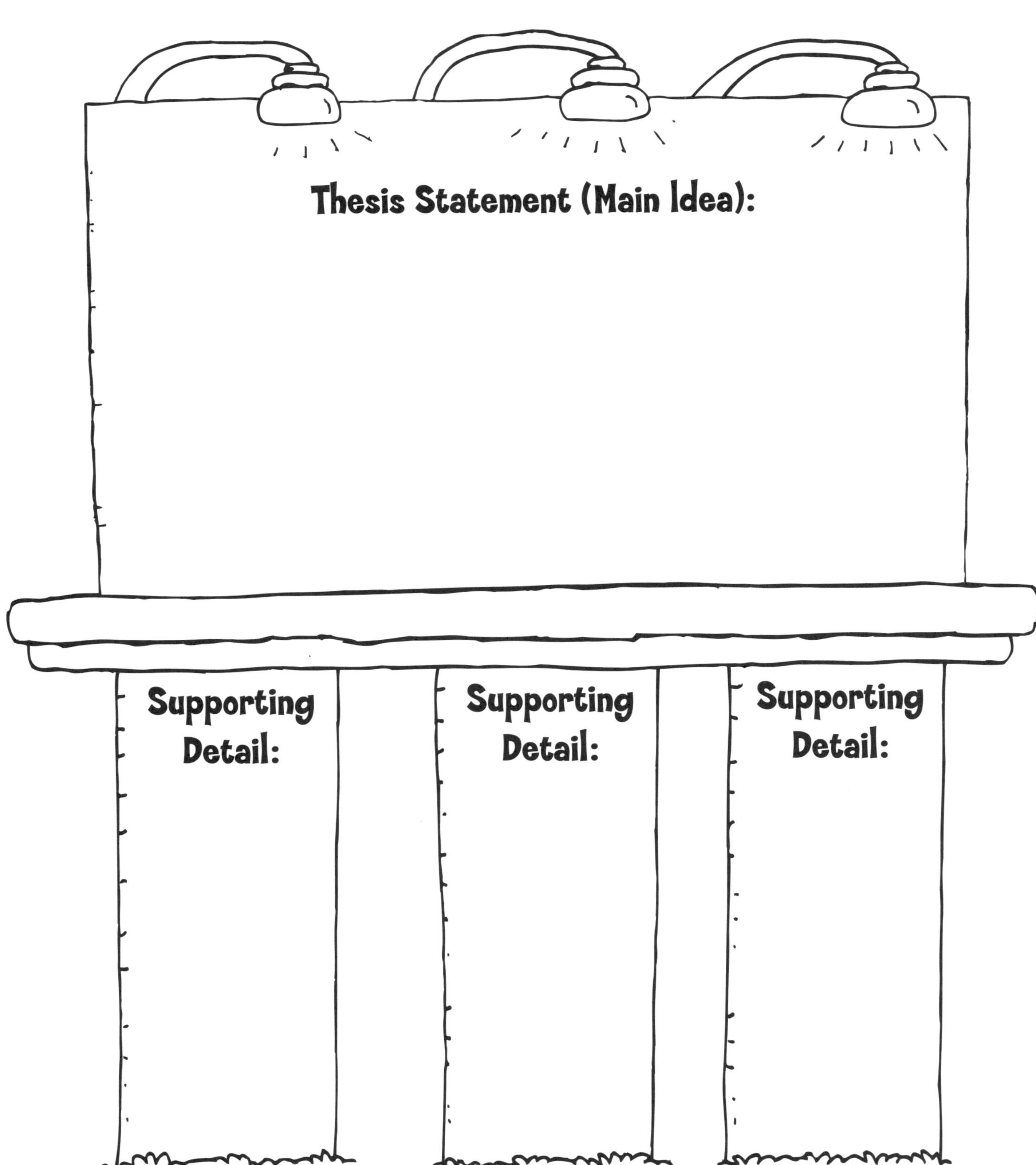

The Idea Factory Graphic Organizer

Name:

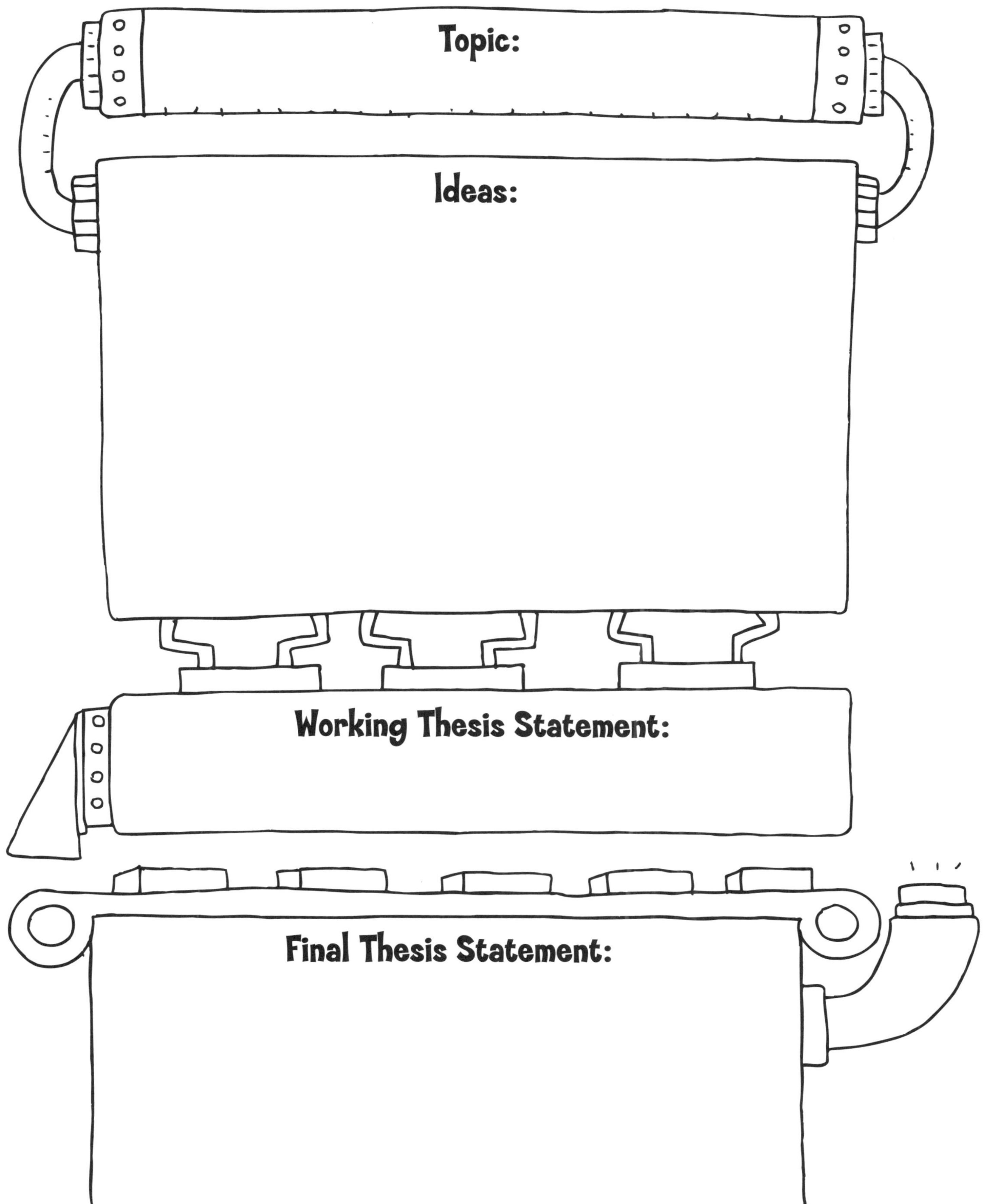

Directions: Buy It Now!

Individual ●

Reproduce "Super Stars" on page 47 or "Ocean Shore Fun Park" on page 48 for each student. Have students study the ad, then answer the questions. When all students are finished, talk about the activity as a class. Explain that the answer to #1 is the main idea of the ad, while the answers to #2 are supporting details.

Small Group ●●

Divide the class into groups of three or four. Reproduce "Super Stars" or "Ocean Shore Fun Park" for each group. Encourage group members to discuss the two questions and write their answers. Then, have students imagine the ad as a radio announcement. Challenge them to use the answers to their questions to describe the ad as if it were being read over the radio. Tell them to write this description down. Invite each group to read its radio ad aloud. Encourage class members to notice how they used the main idea and supporting details to write their radio ads.

Whole Class ●●●

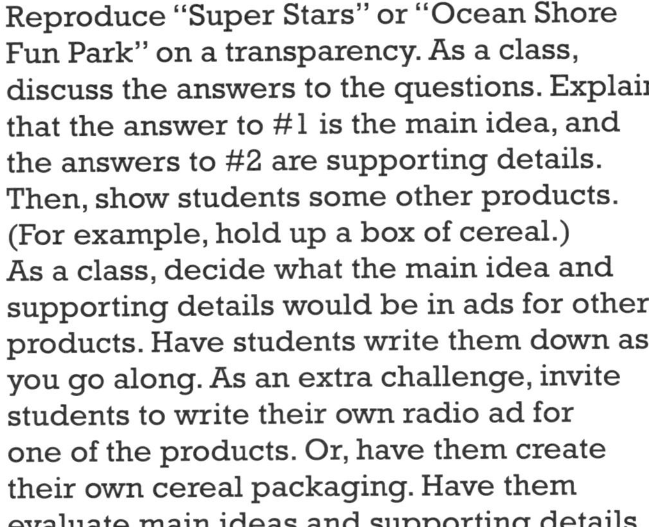

Reproduce "Super Stars" or "Ocean Shore Fun Park" on a transparency. As a class, discuss the answers to the questions. Explain that the answer to #1 is the main idea, and the answers to #2 are supporting details. Then, show students some other products. (For example, hold up a box of cereal.) As a class, decide what the main idea and supporting details would be in ads for other products. Have students write them down as you go along. As an extra challenge, invite students to write their own radio ad for one of the products. Or, have them create their own cereal packaging. Have them evaluate main ideas and supporting details on each other's cereal boxes.

As an extension, show students magazine or newspaper advertisements. Encourage them to name the main ideas and supporting ideas presented. Invite them to critique the legitimacy of the claims.

Answer Key

"Super Stars" (Page 47)

1. You will have energy all morning from the whole grains.
2. They are crunchy, tasty, and healthy.

"Ocean Shore Fun Park" (Page 48)

1. Every day is a holiday at the park.
2. You can bring friends, go on rides, play games, eat food, and win prizes.

Name:

1. What is the main reason to eat Super Stars?

2. What are some other reasons to eat Super Stars?

Ocean Shore Fun Park

Name: ____________________

1. What is the main reason to visit Ocean Shore Fun Park?

2. What are some other reasons to visit Ocean Shore Fun Park?